Taking Your Show on the Road: A Guide for New Student Recruiters

Helen Linstrum

Council for Advancement and Support of Education

In 1974, the American Alumni Council (founded in 1913) and the American College Public Relations Association (founded in 1917) merged to become the Council for Advancement and Support of Education (CASE).

Today, approximately 2,900 colleges, universities, and independent elementary and secondary schools in the U.S. and 20 countries belong to CASE. This makes ours the largest nonprofit 501(c)(3) education association in terms of institutional membership. Representing the member institutions in CASE are more than 13,500 individual professionals in institutional advancement.

Nonprofit education-related organizations such as hospitals, museums, libraries, cultural or performing arts groups, public radio and television stations, or foundations established for public elementary and secondary schools may affiliate with CASE as Educational Associates. Commercial firms that serve the education field may affiliate as Subscribers.

CASE's mission is to advance understanding and support of education for the benefit of society. Central to its mission are its member colleges, universities, and independent schools. CASE fulfills this mission by providing services to beginning, mid-level, and senior advancement professionals; direct services to member institutions; and public affairs programs that bond higher education to the public interest.

CASE offers books, videotapes, and focus issues of the award-winning monthly magazine, CURRENTS, to professionals in institutional advancement. The books cover topics in alumni administration, communications and marketing, fund raising, management, and student recruitment. For a copy of the catalog, RESOURCES, write to the CASE Publications Order Department, 80 South Early Street, Alexandria, VA 22304. For more information about CASE programs and services, call (202) 328-5900.

Cover illustration by Michael David Brown

Council for Advancement and Support of Education
Suite 400, 11 Dupont Circle, Washington, DC 20036

Contents

Foreword

CASE is pleased to present Helen Linstrum's outreach handbook for faculty, staff, and volunteers who represent their institution "on the road." *Taking Your Show on the Road: A Guide for New Student Recruiters* presents, for the first time, the kind of basic information a new recruiter must know to succeed.

Linstrum addresses a range of everyday problems and situations that new recruiters must consider: what to take to a high school program, how to get there and where to park, what to do if the students don't show up, and so on. Her advice about "motels, meals, and mileage" is perfect for anyone who must travel on institutional business, whatever the purpose.

A glossary of "buzz words you need to know" and "tough situations and how to handle them" can help recruiters prepare for the tight spots.

Linstrum is uniquely qualified to write this book: She spent 15 years traveling on outreach assignments for Cal Poly and has been actively involved in the university's on-campus outreach program of counselor conferences, transfer student days, campus tours, and outreach training programs for faculty and staff.

This handbook will help recruiters represent their college or university with integrity while they provide the accurate and timely information students need to get through their "year of decision."

Gary H. Quebl
President, CASE
January 1990

Introduction

This handbook is written for faculty, staff, and volunteers who are involved in counseling college-bound young people and advising the parents, counselors, and teachers who work with them.

The information and suggestions offered here are intended not as a comprehensive course in becoming an outreach specialist, but as a guide to help you help students, while representing your college or university with integrity.

Throughout this text, I will often refer you to your institution's outreach office by which I mean that office that has primary recruiting responsibility on your campus. Your institution may call it "relations with schools," "school and college relations," "admissions," or some other term, but whatever its name, it coordinates your institution's efforts to reach out to prospective students.

Background

Each year, thousands upon thousands of students file applications for admission to one, or several, of the more than 3,000 colleges and universities in the United States. Those students have real concerns about which college to choose, which major to select, how much it will cost, and, scariest of all, what they want to be when they grow up.

Many of these students are attempting to make critically important decisions without much help. Those school districts that have high school counselors don't have enough, and it is difficult for high school or community college counselors to keep abreast of current developments at all the public and private institutions in their own state, let alone at the many institutions across the country.

Parents, anxious to provide guidance, often feel frustrated and diminished by this "year of decision." Many parents have not attended college themselves and can't give guidance from their own personal experience. Some are antagonistic to the idea of a son or daughter leaving home to become more educated and "different" from the rest of the family.

In the end, the most available sources of advice for aspiring collegians are those least qualified to give it—a friend, a cousin who graduated in '72, a teacher who's had no contact with the institution in question, and so on.

Students and their parents need accurate and timely information about college in general and about the specific campuses to which they may be attracted.

Many families, especially those whose socioeconomic position, racial iden-tification, or lack of education makes them feel excluded from the mainstream of society, need much more than the basic information. They need encourage-ment, empathy, and specific and timely facts; most important, they need to know *why* they should allow a precious son or daughter to leave home and enter into a world they don't really understand. That's where we admissions and outreach professionals can make our greatest contribution. If you want to change lives and have a positive impact upon the world, this is the place!

As outreach professionals, our role in life is:

• to enlighten students and their parents about the benefits of a college education and the available means of acquiring it;

• to disseminate to prospective applicants and their parents, teachers, and counselors specific and accurate information concerning admission, financial aid, academic programs, and campus life at our college or university;

• to help students evaluate alternatives and understand more clearly the variety of options open to them; and

• to help prospective students prepare for enrollment.

As we are doing all that, it's important to remember:

• We are working to serve the best interests of the student.

• We are working to complement the services already provided by the high schools and community colleges.

• We speak only of what we know, we look up what we don't know, or we refer questions to knowledgeable others.

• We work most effectively when we coordinate our efforts with those of other segments of our institution.

Chapter 1

Your Role as an Outreach Representative

W hether you are a full-time outreach professional (admissions counselor) for Excellence University or just "hitting the road" once in a while, you'll enjoy the game more if you know how it's supposed to be played.

Whether you are a staff member or a volunteer, you represent not only your department, but your institution and higher education in general. Your job is to provide information and guidance to the students. You're not only a recruiter, you're a counselor. If you do that well, the students you meet who belong at Excellence U. will enroll there and will probably stay. Those who would be better off at another kind of campus are not well served by being recruited to yours.

Try to keep a lot of objectivity in your conversations with students. Don't let preconceived notions creep in. It's important to listen carefully and be sensitive to the students' special interests, priorities, and level of sophistication. And try not to impose your own values and opinions on the students. If they ask you for an opinion, be frank: Tell what you think but remind them that it's only your opinion and leave it up to them to agree or not.

As a representative of Excellence U., you should have in your head at least the basic information about the institution. Even if you are "on the road" rarely or are filling in for someone else, you should know what the university's admission policies are, what kind of financial aid is available and what the basic criteria are for dispensing it, what kind of class configurations a student can expect (class size, availability of professors, and so on), and, especially, what Excellence U.'s central mission is—liberal arts, polytechnic, preprofessional, and so on.

However, you are not expected to know *all* the answers. The trick is to recognize what you know and what you don't. As a campus representative, you shouldn't be drawn into a detailed discussion of matters that fall outside your own field of expertise. If the questions begin going beyond the category of "general," it would be wise for you to refer them to the appropriate office. It's far better to delay answering a question than to answer it incompletely or inaccurately. But the student needs to have the answer eventually—if not immediately—so *do* follow up when you get back to campus. Either research the question and call the student yourself, or refer the question to the staff of your outreach office so they can follow through on it.

If it seems as though you're referring more questions than you're answering, don't worry about it. You're out there fielding them, and that's what counts. The cardinal rule is: *Be prepared.* Have the appropriate literature on hand, as well as plenty of information request cards to allow for systematic follow-up by the staff at home.

These are the basics. The rest of this guide deals with facts you need to know and tips for your survival and success.

Chapter 2

The Image:
You *Are* Excellence U.

L et's assume that you know all you need to know about the university, its programs, and its people, and that you're prepared to give a smashing verbal accounting of all this to your audience. There's still the little matter of image. Will your audience believe what you say?

Think of it this way. A lot of the students and parents with whom you'll be talking will know only one thing about Excellence U.—that Excellence U. chose *you* to represent it to the public. And long after they've forgotten all your information and your good advice, they're going to remember whether or not you seemed like a classy person—especially if you didn't.

Now, let's talk about image. Did you know that when you walk into a room, before you even say "hello," you tell everyone enough about yourself to fill a short book? It's true. Check it out on the next stranger you see. You can make some pretty good guesses as to that person's age, income, occupation, state of mind, self-esteem, taste in clothes, approachability, and so on. That's what makes people-watching so much fun. Of course, it's somewhat disconcerting to realize that *you* are part of a people-watcher's entertainment! But you probably are, more often than you think. And while you're out there representing the institution that hired you, the impressions you're giving of yourself are also the impressions you are giving of your institution and your profession. So with boundless faith in your enlightened self-interest, I'd like to make some suggestions I hope you'll follow.

1. Dress appropriately. Dress like a conservative and successful business-person. The parents with whom you'll be talking are accustomed to that look; many of them have it. Your credibility is enhanced if *you* have it. For men, that means a conservative business suit, black shoes, and dark socks. You may enjoy more colorful clothes, and you're certainly entitled to them. But "on the road," you're a sales representative for Excellence U., and you might recall that IBM hasn't done badly with its blue suit/white shirt dress code. For daytime programs, wool slacks or nice cords and a sports jacket are fine, but evening programs involving parents really do call for the suit. For women, skirted suits or conservative dresses are appropriate, always with hose and reasonably dressy shoes (not too high; you're going to be on your feet a *lot*).

The "corporate image" is never inappropriate, whether you are recruiting aggies, athletes, or astronauts. That look *epitomizes* credibility and competence.

2. Look good. It should go without saying that everything you're wearing will be clean, neat, and in good repair. *You* always keep your stuff that way because you can't stand it otherwise. Right?

3. Smell good. Another personal item—breath mints are a wonderful thing to have around, especially if you smoke or drink coffee or eat pizza for lunch. In a crowded, noisy gym, you have to stand eight inches from your listener to be heard. (Don't offer a breath mint to your listener, though. That's tacky.) Chewing gum, incidentally, is o-u-t. And nothing covers up the aroma of alcohol on your breath, so please skip it until the day is entirely over.

4. Be on time. Whether you are the star attraction or one of the crowd, your presence (or absence) is noted. Promptness is essential. Nothing you have to say will be taken at its full value if people have had to wait too long to hear you say it.

5. Set up attractively. If a table is provided, set it up attractively. Keep it neat and well-stocked. At some college fairs, all you ever see of most of the kids is hands reaching through the crowd to grab your literature. So be vigilant, but don't let your concern for the decor get in the way of your conversation.

6. Introduce yourself to the people in charge. They may be too busy to seek you out, but if you go looking for them, they may remember the questions they've been wanting to ask you. At any rate, they'll remember your good manners. If you can find them when it's time to leave, thank them for inviting you and tell them you enjoyed their program—even if you didn't particularly. They worked hard on it.

If it should happen that you think the hosts blew it in some way, there's no need to tell them (unless they forgot to give you a table, or set you up in a corridor that also serves as a wind tunnel). If they give you an evaluation sheet, you can indicate your criticism *gently* on that. If you do, it helps to have some suggestions for dealing with the problem. Don't just say it was awful and drop it there. In any case, be sure to tell your outreach office when you return to campus. The office may have a standard evaluation form to submit to the errant hosting campus, or perhaps someone more familiar with the individuals involved can tactfully deliver your message.

7. Introduce yourself to the other campus reps, especially those from your system or area. If you're going to be traveling much, these folks can be your buddies, helpers, mentors, and friends. And you need friends on the road.

8. Stay alert. It's sometimes difficult to extricate yourself from one conversation to undertake another, but you should at least indicate to a waiting student that you know he or she is there and you'll get to him or her as soon as possible. You don't want anyone leaving your table in disgust and frustration.

9. Help your colleagues' campuses. If you don't have a particular major, or if you have it but only a few superstars can get into it, refer the inquiring student to another campus that has it available. This helps the student, helps the other campus, and proves you're a nice person and a good counselor. Besides, if you display a generous attitude, other reps will be willing to send students your way too.

10. Stay till it's over. If you are the whole show, this is hard to avoid. But sometimes it's tempting to leave a big program, because you're tired or hungry or your favorite show is on TV back at your hotel room. Don't do it. Your campus expects you to be like Caesar's wife—beyond reproach. Of course, if the program is scheduled to last until 9 p.m. but by 8:30, the only people left are a few campus reps talking to each other, you may go.

11. Save your energy. If you try to do campus visits or a college fair all morning, play golf all afternoon, do a college night in the evening, and party all night, you're not going to last through Tuesday! These programs demand a lot of physical and psychic energy—not to mention the damage done to body and soul by constant traveling, sleeping in strange places, eating irregularly, and just being away from home. So plan your days carefully and don't over-extend yourself.

In a Nutshell

1. Dress appropriately.
2. Look good.
3. Smell good.
4. Be on time.
5. Set up attractively.
6. Introduce yourself to the people in charge.
7. Meet the other reps.
8. Stay alert.
9. Help your colleagues' institutions when you can.
10. Stay till it's over.
11. Save your energy.

Chapter 3

What Is a College Fair (and What Am I Doing Here)?

The term "college fair" can be applied to almost any happening that involves prospective college students and some kind of representatives from two or more institutions of higher learning. If you stay in this business for a while and if you're even a little adventurous with your time and travel budget, you will probably experience a fascinating variety of programs with that festive and ambiguous title.

But for our purposes here, let's stick to those programs that are sponsored by well-intentioned and competent people for the purpose of providing interested youngsters with an opportunity to learn firsthand about as many colleges as possible.

In some parts of the country, a college fair is aimed at high school students and, in most cases, their parents. These events may be held during the day or evening, or they may run for several days. Some are organized by school districts, some by private individuals or groups. In some cases, college representatives are hosted by the sponsoring group; in other cases, participating colleges are expected to pay for the privilege of being represented.

The size of a college fair depends upon several factors:
• the size of the population center in which it is located;
• the effectiveness of the advertising campaign used to publicize it;
• the prevalence of college-oriented families in the area; and
• the judgment of the sponsors as to how big it *should* be.

I have participated in college fairs ranging in size from about 10 families in attendance to crowd scenes of 4,000 people or more. A large crowd does not necessarily equal success, but those numbers give you a reasonable idea of the possibilities you have to consider.

In California, there are two main types of college fairs, and, with the conviction that between them, they probably include most of the essential elements of the genus, I'm going to tell you about them. Besides, if your state doesn't have an organized system for college fairs, you might be interested in adopting or adapting ours. It works very well for us.

The CCUD (California College and University Day)

The two vast systems of public higher education in California are both mandated to provide upper-division education to eligible students who have completed their lower-division studies in one of our 106 community colleges. California's private universities also depend somewhat on upper-division enrollments. So the successful transfer of community college students to one of the university systems is a high-priority responsibility for California's outreach professionals. With that in mind, we developed the world-famous CCUD.

A CCUD (California College and University Day) is a program hosted by a community college, to which representatives from California's many four-year institutions are invited for the purpose of imparting information about their institutions to the students of the community college, so they may all transfer to their favorite universities with a minimum of hassle and confusion. The CCUDs are held in the morning, usually for about four hours. They are publicized by the hosting institution and often include local high school students, bused to the campus especially for the event.

To avoid the appalling prospect of California's 106 community colleges just going off willy-nilly and throwing CCUDs any time they feel like it, the CCUDs are organized statewide by volunteers from two university outreach offices—one in the north and one in the south. (If your state is less than 1,000 miles long, you might get away with only one coordinating office.)

Since all the community colleges want to have their CCUDs at approximately the same time (in the fall when their students begin considering the next step), and since the representatives of the universities can't be everywhere at once, a mutually satisfactory schedule is worked out and distributed by the two outreach offices. Each university then provides one traveling representative for the northern programs and a second "roadrunner" for the southern ones. Actually there may be as many as half-a-dozen folks filling these roles, but usually only two at a time.

Within each segment of the state (north and south), the CCUDs are scheduled so that, within a given week, five community colleges in the same geographic region will host their programs on consecutive days. For example, a typical week might include CCUDs at American River College, Sacramento City College, Consumnes River College, Sierra College, and San Joaquin Delta College. All of these are in Sacramento or within 50 miles of it. Thus the university representatives participating in these programs may do so without an excessive amount of driving in between. This is a blessing, as you will see later.

If you are representing your college or university at a CCUD, you are not normally expected to give a formal speech or presentation. You simply stand at a table which has been provided for you in the campus cafeteria, quad, student lounge, or wherever, and on which you have artfully arranged a custom-made blanket with your school colors and mascot clearly displayed, along with a writing tablet, information request cards, and your most appealing campus promotional literature, and *you talk to students*—all kinds of students with all kinds of questions. They've been waiting weeks for you to show up so they could ask those questions. So you'd better know the answers—or know who does. And unless you're blessed with total recall, you'd better write down the questions to refer to experts on your return to campus or have the students write them on your information request cards.

If the program is a good one, the students' counselors will also stop by to chat and to ask you questions. *They* can come up with some real beauties! Again, you need solid answers. If you don't have them, promise to ask the appropriate person or people on campus. Then *do it* as soon as you get home, and get the answers right back to that counselor yourself. Or ask your outreach staff to handle it for you—they will probably be glad to do it. Of such gestures are good public relations made.

The College Night

The CCUD's companion piece is the High School District College Night or the College Night—a better nickname than HSDCN.

College Nights are scheduled by the northern and southern outreach offices to coincide with the CCUDs in their neighborhoods. They are planned, executed, and hosted by the staff and/or PTA of the participating school district or, possibly, just the hosting high school. The purpose of the College Night is to take advantage of the presence of all those knowledgeable college representatives in town for the CCUD and to give them an opportunity to talk with the students, parents, and, we hope, counselors of the local high school district.

The main difference between a CCUD and a College Night (there are several) is size. Whereas at a very good CCUD, you might make contact with 150 potential transfer students in a four-hour period, at the *typical* College Night, you will have contact with several hundred high school students and their parents within a two- or three-hour period. That is, you will actually speak to or make eye contact with several hundred of the 2,000 to 4,000 who will be there.

College Nights are usually held in high school gymnasiums, which tips you off upfront as to the numbers of people expected to attend. Again, you are expected to stand by your designated table, look approachable, and answer all kinds of questions. The high school students' questions are generally not as sophisticated as those of the community college students, so sometimes you need to think beyond what they ask and tell them what they need to know. Not too much, though. If you begin to notice their eyes glazing over—stop. And *do* be gracious to their proud and effusive parents. Remember that, while Johnny may be just another kid to you, he is the hope and light of their lives, so let them tell you what a great kid he is and how deserving of admission to your institution. After all, he is!

At a College Night, you may be asked to give a speech about Excellence U. to a group of particularly interested parents and students. If this is going to happen, you will *probably* be warned ahead of time—but not necessarily. I walked into a College Night once and spotted a sign on the wall announcing that the Cal Poly rep would speak in Room 118 at 7:20. Since it was then 7:10, it was a *very* extemporaneous speech. This can happen at any time, so have your presentation outline at the ready.

College Nights are both good news and bad news. The good news is that they provide the kids with broad exposure to all kinds of institutions in the form of real, live representatives as well as attractive literature to look at. They allow parents to get the straight story from the people who know. They allow for on-the-spot comparisons among the various institutions in which a young-ster might be interested. And I've noticed they provide a wonderful social opportunity for families who haven't seen each other for months.

The bad news is that, with so *much* information available in one place, students often just cruise the area, picking up every piece of paper they can find, and not taking advantage of the opportunity to get firsthand answers to their own concerns or to explore the different options. Some College Night programs look somewhat like a Friday night basketball game without the basketball; the students seem to be there primarily to see and be seen, and the college search is merely a sideline. Or sometimes there are so many people asking questions and demanding a representative's attention that nobody can get very much of it, so questions that might be important go unasked, and the reps sometimes get a little harried, trying to handle so many people at the end of a long day, a long week, or a long season. So it's important to keep your poise and take afternoon naps if you need them to stay cheerful. Just be careful not to nap while you're driving from one town to another!

The Special

The third type of program in which you will become involved is the Excellence U. Special. This is when you or another campus rep visits individual high schools during the school day. It is sometimes at their request, but more often at yours.

Unlike a CCUD or College Night where you are surrounded by colleagues from other institutions and where you chat with whoever comes along, a Special program is just *you*. And you *are* going to make a presentation. That's why you're there. And unlike the big programs where the hosting school staff are, to some extent, staking their own reputations on the success of the program (which means they're going to make sure the kids show up), an Excellence U. Special is just one of many visits by many college reps to a particular school. So the counselor or career center technician who made the appointment with you may or may not be impressed with his or her good fortune at having the Excellence U. presence descend upon the scene.

This means you may have 30 interested juniors and seniors showing up at the appointed hour to hang on your every word and ask you intelligent, well-informed questions. Or you may get zero, and the counselor not even around to take the blame. Or, hardest of all, the counselor may be there to introduce you proudly to four or five slightly bored students who straggle in and out, one by one, throughout the appointed hour, chat with the counselor and each other, and leave you in a quandary as to whether you should try to give your prepared talk, confine yourself to answering the same questions four or five times, or just sit there exuding charm and approachability (through clenched teeth).

The best advice is to roll with the punches, do your best to give them the most information you can, and keep your cool. Counselors have their problems too, and not all schools are efficiently run. But you probably don't need to mention that. You might tactfully suggest that you can be most effective if all the kids come at once so you can tell them *all* the good things you know to help them make a wise choice. (This should probably be done during the initial appointment call, but it may bear repeating.)

If *nobody* shows up, don't give up in disgust. Spend a few minutes with the counselor, the career center technician, the volunteer parent in the library—*anyone* who has access to the students and who might like to have some information to pass on. Tell that person some provocative fact about your institution. Get a little conversation going. Then—before you've outstayed your welcome—generously leave a supply of your best stuff (you brought it along for this school, anyway), thank your listener for his or her time, and go away. This is not the time to try to find out why their kids don't seem to like Excellence U. The person you're talking to probably doesn't know. If he or she does know, you aren't likely to find out unless you ask. And asking, I'm afraid, no matter how you do it, sounds a little whiney. Besides, that may not be the problem at all.

Whatever the reason, if your visit to any school turns out to be a bust, let your outreach office know so that staff can either replow that field or give it a rest for a while. When setting up individual visits, the outreach office should try to determine that:

• the students have some interest in your institution;

11

• there are no conflicting events taking place that day; and
• the counselor will be there.

But sometimes the counselors forget or an unknowing algebra teacher will schedule a last-minute exam. Don't take it personally. Most high schools are delighted—or at least willing—to have you visit, so your next appointment is bound to be a good one.

Keeping in touch with outreach

There are more ways to represent Excellence U. than those I've described. If you are representing your academic department to students in a corresponding department at a community college or high school; if you are a student going back to your high school to give your university a plug; if you are an alum bent on selling your alma mater to some of the most talented kids you know, your outreach office would be interested in knowing your plans beforehand and hearing of your experiences when you come back.

This is probably the place to mention that your outreach office is responsible for coordinating *all* outreach activities from your campus. If you insist on going it alone, no one will grab you by the ankles and beg you to stay home. But outreach probably keeps a schedule of who's going where; staff members know what materials will be needed when you get there; they know the answers to a lot of questions; and they're probably very nice people. So I urge you to coordinate your visits with them. They can help you avoid embarrassing situations like being the third Excellence U. person to visit the same school in one week, or showing up with 50 applications when the school counselor was hoping for freshman admission guides and viewbooks. *And* they can get answers for all those tough questions that get thrown at you. That's their job, and they're more than happy to help you in whatever ways they can.

In a Nutshell

1. *Stand* at your table.
2. Be approachable and friendly. Smile!
3. Know your stuff.
4. Refer what you don't know. Don't guess.
5. Get tough questions in writing, with names and phone numbers.
6. Follow through.
7. Listen for the real question behind the words.
8. Be prepared to give a speech if appropriate.

9. Maintain your poise.
10. Keep the outreach office informed before and after your trip.
11. Read this checklist before each program.

Chapter 4

Getting There
Is Half the Fun

I t has been my experience that making an appointment to visit an individual
high school is a five-phone-call activity. There's the initial call: The party
you're calling is in conference and can he or she return your call? The
return call comes; *you* are in conference. You make the third call; your party
is in, but has to consult before setting a time. On the fourth call, he or she has
a time, but you're out of your office and can't confirm. On call five, you finally
connect and the appointment is set.

If you understand that the process works this way, you can avoid a lot of
frustration. However, since you're probably trying to set up compatible appointments at several different schools, and you have plenty of other things to do
with your time, you'll probably be happier if you delegate this chore to a
careful, pleasant, patient other person.

Your outreach office probably has a list of contact persons at each high
school and community college in your service area. If you don't already have
a special contact at a given school, outreach staff will be glad to steer you to
theirs. It's a lot easier and more productive to start with someone who knows
your institution than to just take whoever is free when you call.

Your school visit evaluation form (we call it a trip sheet) should have a space
for directions to your destination from the nearest major highway. Whoever
makes your appointment should get that information from a confident, *adult*
person at the school you're planning to visit. It makes good sense for the
person at your end to read the directions back over the phone to make sure
they're right. Then—unless they're so clear that this would be embarrassing—
call the day of the visit and confirm them. I'm not kidding about this. Because
I didn't take this extra step, I've seen more of Oxnard, Modesto, and Shafter

15

than any tourist needs to see. If you think, as I did, that a little town with 2,500 people can't possibly hide its high school from you, think again!

Having taken these cumbersome precautions, *allow yourself twice as much time as you think necessary to reach the school*. Better to sit in the parking lot for 20 minutes going over your notes and trying not to look sinister than to arrive out of breath and flustered, scattering papers in your wake, halfway through your designated speaking time. There is an immutable law that decrees that if you try to skin it too close, you will encounter road construction, 17 red lights, and a slow-moving freight train on your way to the school.

Another item you should know about before you arrive is *where to put the car*. It is a blessed thing—and rare—to find a high school with a big, open parking lot clearly visible in front of the administration building. And your day will not be made by dragging a rickety pull-cart with 87 pounds of paper from one corner of a campus to the other, past the football field, over the speed bumps, and through two corridors lined with open-doored classrooms, especially if you didn't follow the previous advice and you're late. So *ask* when the appointment is made, and write down the answer. Never trust your memory on the road. (If you insist on being independent and finding your own parking place, look for the flagpole. The administration is usually close by and you can at least ask someone there if there's a spare parking space for you.)

The third thing you need to know before you arrive is who is going to present you to your audience. Get the name, spelled correctly, on your trip sheet, and try to be sure you know how to pronounce it. You know how you resent people who mess up your name. Check it before you step into the school so you can say it to whoever greets you. "I have an appointment with Ms. Czisawolski in the Career Center" is so much more impressive than "I'm supposed to see—uh—Ms.—uh—the counselor."

Sometimes, through no fault of yours, Ms.—uh—the counselor has flown the coop for the day and has, you may hope, made arrangements for you to meet your audience in some obscure classroom without any help from her. You may properly be offended by this, since she knew you were coming and should have mentioned that she'd be gone. But try to take it like a trooper and do your job anyway, even if she's being lax in doing hers. Strange as it may seem, our visits are not *always* the high point in a counselor's week. Usually, but not always.

The last item you must know before you leave home is the phone number of the school you'll be visiting. You'll need it to confirm your directions (remember?), and you never know what might happen. The transmission may fall out of your rented car on the way; you could wake up on the day of your visit with the world's worst cold. And there's one thing we absolutely *never* do. We never just don't show up! So have the phone number in the car, and if disaster strikes and you can't make it, call the people at the school and let them know. Otherwise, you can be sure that they'll remember the day the Excellence

U. person didn't show up even longer than you'll remember the day Ms.—uh—the counselor took the afternoon off.

If your visit is to a college fair or a high school night, chances are you will receive a map and a letter from a real person with a name and a telephone number. Guard them with your life until you get to the program! And please return them to your outreach office when you get home, in case the next representative to that program doesn't get any.

In a Nutshell

1. Start arranging your visit well ahead of time.
2. Use established contacts.
3. Confirm directions and parking arrangements.
4. Allow plenty of time to get there.
5. Know your contact's name.
6. Keep directions and phone number at hand.

Chapter 5

Buzz Words You Need to Know

E very profession has its jargon and in a field like ours, where the products (college graduates) are the result of the efforts of many subgroups, everyone needs at least a passing acquaintance with the subjargons that evolve. In other words, you need to know what you're saying when you're saying it. Otherwise, you can get yourself, the university, and, worst of all, the student in a very bad spot.

In some books, this section would be called a glossary. But a lot of people never look at a glossary, and I wanted to be sure you looked at these terms, so I sneaked the whole thing in here, hoping to catch your attention. Don't try to memorize these terms. Just keep this section handy when you're away from home so you can refer to it as needed.

A.A. degree (Associate of Arts): an intermediate degree awarded by junior colleges and community colleges after two years of directed lower-division studies; thought by many students to be required for transfer to a university, it usually isn't.

Achievements (Achievement Tests): required for admission by the University of California as well as many private and public universities; available in specific subject areas and administered by the Educational Testing Service (ETS) of the College Board.

ACT (American College Test): a standardized admission test given nationwide and required for freshman admission by many universities, especially in the central part of the U.S. Most colleges require and accept either the ACT or SAT (see below) for freshman and lower-division applicants, while strongly recommending one or the other for upper-division applicants.

APs (Advanced Placement Tests): a series of tests administered by ETS through which students can receive college credit for college-level work undertaken in high school. A score of 3, 4, or 5 is required by most colleges to receive advanced placement and/or college credit.

Articulation Agreement: a list of course equivalencies or recommended courses between two- and four-year institutions to facilitate transfer. Not all colleges maintain agreements with other institutions, but, combined with some guidance, these agreements can be very helpful to prospective transfer students.

A.S. degree (Associate of Science): see A.A. degree above.

Campus rep: outreach representative for a college or university (you!).

Career Certificate (Technical Certificate): a terminal award given to students who have completed a course of study leading directly to employment in a technical or vocational field. Ordinarily the courses taken to earn a career certificate are not transferable to a university; unfortunately, many students assume they are.

Career Day: similar to a college night, but includes representatives of career areas that don't require college; may feature beauty salons giving free haircuts or forest rangers handing out free baby trees. Free counseling may not be a big attraction.

CLEP (College Level Entry Program): a series of tests given by the College Board by which a person can gain college credit without taking courses. Universities vary in their policies regarding acceptance of these tests, so check with yours.

Confirmation of Admission: the final notice of admission sent to a student after his or her transcripts and test scores have been seen, evaluated, and approved.

Equivalent courses: community college courses that have been designated as matching up with specific lower-division university courses through an articulation agreement. Transfer applicants often ask about transferable courses; they should be told about equivalent courses as well. They often don't know there's a difference.

GE (General Education and Breadth requirements, GEB, General Ed, Gen Ed, General Studies): required at most colleges, they cover several curricular areas and are intended to expose the student to the broad range of ideas that comprise our culture.

High School Equivalency: a test that, if passed, indicates that the student knows all that's necessary to graduate from high school. Check your campus policy in regard to admission of applicants who have completed high school in this manner. Another version of this is the G.E.D. or General Education Diploma.

Impacted program (oversubscribed major): a major course of study for which there are more qualified applicants than can be admitted. Since popularity is what made these programs impacted, you can expect a lot of questions about them. It's a good idea to have some basic answers, such as general admission requirements, but you'll probably be doing a lot of referring or researching on these.

International Baccalaureate: a diploma awarded to secondary school students after the 13th year of study. In some cases, one year of college credit may be awarded to holders of this diploma.

"On the Road Again": the theme song of outreach representatives, recorded by Willie Nelson with our tacit permission and with great profit for him.

Oversubscribed major: another term for an impacted program. The term "oversubscribed" is preferred; it is more readily understood and less painful.

Receiving institution: the college or university to which a student is transferring from his or her original college.

Roadrunner: university representative, outreach/campus representative, mobile admissions counselor.

SAT (Scholastic Aptitude Test): standardized college entrance exam administered by ETS and normally required of freshman applicants to nearly every university; often interchangeable with the ACT.

Seventh semester transcript: the official transcript of grades from the first half of the senior year of high school; required for final admission to most universities, although some require the sixth, seventh, and/or eighth, depending upon selectivity.

Transferable units (transferable courses): those units or courses that a college has determined to be baccalaureate level and leading toward a bachelor's degree; not necessarily equivalent to anything at the receiving institution.

Chapter 6

Tough Situations and How to Handle Them

Y ou've probably noticed that just when you think you've heard it all, you find there's a never-ending well of creativity out there, and the *wildest* questions seem to bubble up from it all the time. They're most likely to hit you in public with at least a dozen people hanging on your response.

For this reason, I encourage you—I urge you—to take some time to read the various materials about Excellence U. and its programs. You may be surprised at how much you didn't know, thought you knew but were wrong about, never thought of, never even heard of, or can't imagine the reason for. It's fascinating to look beyond your own area of interest and see what's out there in someone else's space. And a little time spent in this fashion will give you a broader understanding than you might already have of the truly amazing array of people and interests that we can and do serve within our institutions.

No one would ever expect you to absorb all you read about every program on campus. But by reading the material furnished to you by the outreach office, you can quickly obtain an overall view of the university, and you'll have a clue as to where a student, parent, or counselor might go for help that you can't give them right now.

Here's a list of guidelines to follow when you're on the road, alone and helpless. Failure to abide by these suggestions can result in confiscation of your table blanket and the keys to the university car!

1. Tough questions about admission are best answered by your admissions office. If you are on the admissions office staff, of course you know the answers to everything. If not, you should know the answers to the easy questions before you go out, and the outreach office will do everything possible to see that you do. But no one has ever devised a system for anticipating every question that might surface. So if you're stumped, or if you're not *sure,* get the student's

name and address, have him or her write down the question on the information request card, and ask someone in the admissions office to get back to that person.

This goes for admission to any program or major, including the one you might be representing. There's no use guessing about admissions procedures, priorities, or requirements. Unless your school has a *total and absolute* open-door policy, even a *slightly* wrong answer can mean that the kid you talked to won't be admitted. He or she won't thank you for that. Nor will admissions. If you are *in* admissions or if your institution prefers that one person be the primary contact for each prospective student, you'll have to do some research in admissions and follow through yourself.

2. Never—and I mean *never*—guarantee a student that with his or her GPA and SAT score, admission to a particular program of choice is a cinch. It is not! You really don't know from term to term just exactly what the admissions situation is going to be. If you can stand one more personal example of rash judgment, I'll tell you how I learned this rule the hard way.

Several years ago at a College Night, a young man who could only be described as a superstar asked me about his chances for admission to Cal Poly's computer science major. This boy was good! He had everything Cal Poly hopes for in an applicant, including a GPA of 3.79. "No problem!" I said in my most confident manner. Unfortunately, as it turned out, the cutoff for computer science freshmen that year was 3.87, and my superstar wasn't admitted, and his father, who just happened to be the senior counselor at that high school of 3,000 students, spent 45 minutes on the phone with me trying to understand why his really wonderful son wasn't admitted after I had said he would be. Do you know how bad crow tastes? You will find out if you make promises.

Say, instead, "Excellent chance," or "Looking good," or any encouraging thing that comes to mind (*if* it's justified), but *never* say, "You bet—I guarantee it!" Even if your institution has ordered you to "bring 'em back if they're breathing," you would be better off never to speak in absolutes and guarantees. Besides your institution might add a little lustre to its aura if it doesn't sound all that eager to enroll just *everybody*. (If you happen to be the dean, and you're willing to go out on a limb for this kid, in writing, you may ignore the above. But you'd better remember to write that note!)

3. There will always be arrogant, unpleasant people who just happen to be parents of college-age children. When they approach you with intimidation in their hearts—ignore it. These are not personal attacks. Remember, you are good, you know what you're talking about, you are there to state and explain your institution's policies—not to defend them. Above all, you are not there to defend yourself. You don't need to bow and touch your forelock for these folks, but don't allow them to rile you. There is never any excuse for a campus rep to be hostile or offensive. It's our lot to be tactful and civil at all times.

4. If your university enjoys a strong reputation and a selective admissions policy, you are intimately acquainted with the concept of a "mixed blessing."

When your institution rejects a well-qualified applicant, his or her parents will be eager for you to show up at the next school program in their neighborhood. It's to their credit that they never come armed, but they do let you know how they feel—and it's not happy. A very important part of your job as Excellence U.'s representative is to help them and their child accept the institution's decision. Remind them that Excellence U. is not the only game in town, and try to suggest some acceptable alternatives.

It's difficult not to hold out hope for next term for these folks—they are justifiably disappointed. But keep your poise. Tell them what they and their children can do to make things better. *You* can do nothing except suggest some different options.

5. The counselor who has sponsored a nonadmitted student and urged him or her to apply to Excellence U. may be even tougher to handle than the parents. Keep in mind when you're talking to a counselor that:

• Excellence U.'s rejection notice has compromised the counselor's credibility;

• The counselor has had to deal with a disappointed youngster who may blame him or her for this disappointment;

• If the counselor believes the student didn't get a fair consideration, he or she will probably not urge the next likely candidate to apply to your institution.

6. Some high school districts are so successful at publicizing their college nights that the attendant crowd totally overwhelms the available representatives. It is possible for as many as 4,000 people to go through a gymnasium or convention center in the first two hours of a three-hour program. (I've heard of bigger ones, but I don't even want to think about them!) This is very nice for the hosts—clear proof of success. But for the campus reps it can be just *awful.*

The important thing to remember is that people will go *first* to the representative of the campus that interests them most. So try to give the early birds a lot of attention. If you don't have time to really talk with them, invite them to come by your table a little later when things have calmed down a bit. And stay cool. It's· hard to be calm when people are waiting six deep to talk with you, but it's essential. If you get rattled, nobody wins. And think how wonderful it is that your campus is so popular!

7. If you're having the opposite problem—none of those 4,000 people are stopping at your table or even catching your eye—well, I hope that there are some mission and strategy meetings going on back home to address and correct this problem. Or maybe you're just in the wrong part of the country and what your institution has to offer, they're simply not going to want. You could settle for an evening of uninterrupted people-watching, but don't despair yet. You might try a few small tactics since you're here anyway and your evening's pretty well committed.

First of all, stand in front of your table rather than behind it. Make eye contact and smile at the people as they stroll by. (Even if this doesn't work, you may

25

be amused by the different methods people use to avoid meeting your eye. You might even decide to give up recruiting in favor of writing humorous books.) I wouldn't be holding pieces of literature out to them if I were you. That's kind of—um—"circus barkerish." Just smile and if you succeed in catching someone's eye, say hello. Some nice friendly remark about the program or the weather might be appropriate. The point is, you have to sell *you* before they'll be interested in your institution if it's one they've never heard of or never thought about very much.

Remember what I said about image in Chapter 2? If you've taken the time to introduce yourself to the representatives from the more popular campuses, told them a little bit about Excellence U. and what it offers, they may be gracious enough to send some business your way. It's worth a try; you can't lose. At least you will have met some nice colleagues.

8. Last but not least, *never* let yourself be drawn into the "which institution is better" trap. Recommend good programs in the student's area of interest, but remind him or her that each institution has its strengths, and education is the student's responsibility as much as the university's. This admonition is not just to protect you from a potentially unpleasant conversation. There are important ethical issues at work here. Each of us is out there to help students and our university, but we really don't accomplish either by being chauvinistic.

Just because I've only listed eight tough situations, don't think for a minute that that's all there are. The possibilities for difficulty are unlimited. Dealing with people is an unpredictable job at best, so it behooves you always to be as well prepared as possible, leave your cares and your sore feet outside the arena, and enjoy "Showtime!"

In a Nutshell

1. Refer tough admissions questions—in writing—with the student's name and phone number. Or, if your position or institutional policy dictates, follow through yourself.
2. Never promise admission unless you have the official authority to make it happen.
3. Maintain your poise and good manners—no matter what.
4. Be ready with suggestions to help turn disappointment and frustration into productive action.
5. Treat counselors as members of the same team and see that they have all the information you can provide. Refer them to the outreach office when appropriate.
6. Stay calm in crowds. Remember, a crowd is just a lot of individuals.

7. Make yourself as approachable as possible, and your institution will benefit from the interest you inspire.
8. Don't rank one institution against another.
9. A sense of humor is a wonderful thing.

Chapter 7

Following Through

Of course, all the poise and good humor and great information in the world won't get the job done if you don't follow through when you get back to campus. This is hardly ever easy. Unless you have the good fortune to be working for Utopia U., you're facing a stack of top-priority items in your IN basket that have been there since the day you left, and they were all due last week. Some of us routinely spend our first day back in the office just sort of dazedly stirring the pile and trying to decide what *has* to be done tomorrow. The real top priority is usually just trying to get your mind in from the road and back to your desk.

But follow-through is the name of the game, so maybe you could use some hints on how to do it as painlessly as possible.

Remember the writing tablet you kept handy at the various programs? The one on which you wrote the names, addresses, and unanswerable questions of students at these programs? Remember your stack of information request cards? Make those your first priority when you return to your office. Get them out of your traveling bag, put them front and center on your desk, and start chipping away at them.

Contact the appropriate persons who can answer those questions, make certain you understand the answers as they're given to you, and write your letters to each one of those kids.

There are at least three good reasons for doing this job first. One is that you may still remember all or most of the kids who asked the questions, which makes it easier to write a personalized letter to each one of them. The second is that this particular activity almost automatically eases you back into the office mode, making the transition a lot easier on you. A third and more subtle benefit is that while you're doing this all-important follow-up activity, no one (well, almost no one) will really lean on you to get involved in something else that you're not yet ready to face.

Follow-through is also important in terms of the short- and long-range planning efforts of your outreach office. Your institution needs to know some basic things about the schools you visited and the programs in which you participated in order to make decisions regarding future relationships with those schools. And since you were there, you're going to be the one to provide the information.

Now, if outreach staff members have been thinking ahead, they're probably going to provide you with a school visit evaluation form (trip sheet) designed to collect all the necessary information. If they don't offer you such a form, ask for it. If they don't have one, you could do everyone on your campus a big favor by designing one for them.

An evaluation form can help you not only to keep valid statistics and evaluate your visit, but, as you've already seen, it can be a convenient tool in making your appointments.

The trip sheet should have spaces to note all the things you need to know about the school before you go, as well as all the things you and your outreach office need to be aware of when you come back. For example, you should be able to tell from the trip sheet how many students are attending the school you're going to visit, how many applied to Excellence U. for the current year and how many of those were accepted, and how many former students are now attending your university.

It should tell you the address and phone number of the school and the name (and how to pronounce it) and position of the contact person there. And the sheet should include spaces for you to note how many students you talk with at the school, what majors they're interested in, how many belong to under-represented ethnic groups and how many of those students you talk with. There should be plenty of room for you to write in any special concerns voiced by the counseling staff or the students.

If you will take a few moments to fill out your part of the trip sheet before you leave the school or the program, the main part of your follow-up efforts will be done. This is critical. You may think you'll remember the important points later, but you won't. After just one week on the road, all the schools you visited tend to run together. If you're out for two or three weeks, you'll be lucky to remember your middle name by the time you get home.

At a large program where several high schools are represented, it's usually not possible to fill out a separate sheet for each school in attendance. But if you have an evaluation form for each of those schools before you go, at least you'll have a pretty good idea of what to expect and how to prepare. And you can give an evaluation of the program on your trip sheet.

If the outreach staff see an evaluation form indicating that you spoke with 85 interested students and 37 of them were from underrepresented ethnic backgrounds, they're going to do some additional work in that area or at least send you or someone else to that program again next year. If you spoke to only six students and two of them had mistaken you for someone else, maybe your campus will decide to pass on that program next time around.

Whenever you go to any kind of off-campus program, you should be carrying inquiry or information request cards for students to fill out and return to your table or mail back to campus at their convenience. The method of answering these will differ from campus to campus and depend largely on the volume of cards received. If you're part of a reasonably large operation, the response to a student inquiry will probably be a package of preprinted materials that respond to the particular interests of the student who filled out the card. If yours is a smaller institution or the number of inquiries is minimal, your outreach office may prefer that you send a personal letter to each of the students.

Either way, inquiries should be answered *promptly*. If you get a huge volume of inquiries during the travel season, your outreach office may want to hire some additional help (perhaps student assistants) to handle the mail during that period.

Those inquiry cards are useful little things. Besides providing a convenient way for your campus to respond to student interests, they can provide the basis for your prospective applicant tracking system. The tracking system may or may not intersect with your responsibilities, but if your campus is using inquiry cards to track prospective students from first contact to application to enrollment, you can see that the outreach office will be very interested in getting all your inquiry cards into the system. So do try not to lose them in your travels.

The final thing you'll want to do as a follow-up activity is write thank-you notes to the schools that hosted you. Fortunately, this isn't difficult. A thank-you is a thank-you, and there are only so many ways you can say it, so you can have a basic format worked out for repeated use. It's nice, though, to receive a thank-you note that indicates the writer knows who you are, so while you're filling out your evaluation sheet at the school or program, make note of some little individual item that you can mention later on in your note. ("I was particularly impressed with how competently your school handled the fire in the gymnasium during State U.'s presentation!")

You might even want to take some stationery along on your trip and get those thank-you notes written while you watch TV in your hotel room.

You or your campus may include some additional activities in the follow-up process. Or you may follow through in a different way entirely. It really doesn't matter *what* the activities are, as long as your travel means something and can be translated into visible results for your campus and real help for the students you contact.

In a Nutshell

1. Research and write responses to tough student questions.
2. Complete and return your school visit evaluation forms (trip sheets).

3. Follow up on student inquiry (information request) cards; respond and collect for tracking.
4. Write thank-you notes to schools that hosted you.
5. Now tackle that IN basket!

Chapter 8

The Complete Travel Kit

Although a competent, personable *person* is the best outreach device a university can have, students also need something they can take home to look at, so there are a number of items you should have with you wherever you go. Besides, *you* need some things to look at when the questions come thick and fast, and you don't really know the answers.

Every campus has its own package of promotional literature, designed for certain times and audiences. I've seen campus reps loaded down with 100 catalogs for each program—and nothing else. And I've seen others with a dazzling array of four-color brochures for every occasion spread enticingly on their tables (I'd kill for their budgets!).

Most campuses fall between these two extremes, with a few brochures ranging from the purely motivational to the more detailed and instructional. And many campuses have a well-thought-out plan for distributing these in a logical sequence (browsers get the motivational brochure, serious inquirers get the admissions booklet, and so on). If your campus has such a distribution plan, you should make every effort to follow it. If not, I offer you the Cal Poly Travel Kit as a model to adopt or adapt. You may want to rearrange some or all of these items into other categories, or you might eliminate some and add others, but you've got to start somewhere.

So, listed under the headings of "keepers," "giveaways," and "discretionary giveaways," here are the things you need on the road. Incidentally, these items have been placed in their respective categories based on the students' need to know right now and the production cost of each piece.

For College Fairs and College Nights

Keepers

These are the basics:

• a blanket or banner with your university logo to drape over the table where you'll be stationed;

• a university catalog (bring extras so you can be generous to teachers and counselors who've lost theirs);

• an application booklet to be used as a reference;

• a copy of your financial aid or scholarship booklet;

• a list of your athletic teams and coaches, as well as the sports available in your intramural program;

• several copies of your admissions statistics for the previous fall (showing the average GPAs, SAT or ACT scores, and completed coursework of successful applicants); and

• a writing tablet and pen for the tough questions and the names and phone numbers of the people who asked them.

Giveaways

Take a lot of these to put out on the table:

• your introduction brochure (your first contact piece); this is how students get acquainted with you, and everyone who walks by your table should get one;

• inquiry (information request) cards; students fill these out if they want more information (and they usually do); the cards should be designed so they can be returned to you or mailed to the campus (include prepaid postage);

• your guide to admissions which instructs prospective students in the steps to successful enrollment; and

• special-interest brochures paid for by other departments, such as ROTC, Housing, Theater, etc.; this is an opportunity for your recruitment-minded academic departments to advertise their wares.

Discretionary giveaways

These are expensive or in short supply, so keep them under the table, but give them gladly to anyone who asks or who seems genuinely interested in your institution:

• your viewbook;

• a reasonable supply of curriculum/career guides for each major (your outreach office can tell you what's reasonable); and

• special program brochures (e.g., Educational Opportunity Program, Disabled Student Services, Cooperative Education).

For transporting all this material, your outreach office can provide you with carrying cases and a pull-cart. Cardboard boxes and strained muscles are not very impressive, and you can mention that if you run into any resistance when you ask for the cases and cart.

And don't forget to take this guide and your maps and phone numbers!

For Excellence U. Specials

Keepers

The basics:

• your school blanket or banner;

• a copy of your model presentation outline (see the next chapter for more about this very important item);

• a copy of admissions statistics;

• a writing tablet for tough questions and pencils for students to use;

• a trip sheet with directions, telephone numbers, and name of contact person; and

• this guide.

Giveaways

Bring plenty of these (except for the catalog):

• a university catalog (unless you own stock in the company that printed the catalog, give a copy only to your contact person);

• your introduction brochure;

• inquiry (information request) cards;

• your viewbook (to be given away freely at this type of program);

• Excellence U. stickers or other cute promotional gimmicks;

• guide to admissions; and

• special program brochures.

Chapter 9

Your Campus Presentation

Your institution may already have a model presentation as part of its outreach training package. If so, you should learn it thoroughly. If there is no model presentation, here's your chance to make some career points by fashioning one. To give you a hand in this selfless endeavor, I offer you the model for Cal Poly's standard presentation. The model is obviously a pretty sketchy outline; in practice it takes about 18 minutes to deliver. You may be able to give your presentation in less time, but don't take more. Remember, you're dealing with the MTV generation here, and you can't expect them to be thrilled with your voice for a whole hour. (Ask their teachers!) Besides, you have to leave ample time for all those perceptive questions they're going to ask you.

In your model presentation, you should emphasize the uniquely appealing things your campus has to offer. Otherwise, why are you there? At Cal Poly, we know that our top three assets, in the eyes of prospective students, are the attractiveness of our campus and its location (California's central coast); our hands-on philosophy of education, which is associated with our reputation for producing highly employable graduates; and the high level of student involvement inherent in our position as a residential campus (read "friendliness"). You'll notice these points are emphasized in our presentation outline. The emphasis comes across even more clearly as the presentation is delivered.

Another thing to remember here is that you're speaking to a group of individuals with their own personal and group concerns. You'll be infinitely more successful with them if you begin your presentation by showing that you are a warm, caring human being and that you have some interest in them as persons and as members of an important group (seniors at Hectic High School). Here's how we do it at Cal Poly.

Model for Standard Cal Poly Outreach Presentation

I. Introduction of yourself: name, school, position, phone (on board).
Happy to be here (enthusiasm, smile).
Local references: academic excellence, football victory, rodeo day, midterms, etc.

II. Purpose of visit:
Ask about numbers of seniors, juniors, those who've decided on college, applied, been admitted.

Information to help you decide what *you* are looking for in college.
What colleges represented today (or located in the area) have what you may want.

Ask questions of knowledgeable representatives.

III. The California State University system (of which Cal Poly is a part): missions, scope, variety; other higher education opportunities in California (University of California, community colleges, private colleges).

IV. Cal Poly:
Environment: How many of you have visited our campus?
San Luis Obispo: location, climate, ocean, mountains, beauty, ambience.
Demographics: size (6,000-plus acres), enrollment, variety of students, age.

Residential: collegial, on-campus housing almost assured for new students enrolling for fall quarter.

Academic: "Polytechnic" = "many technologies."
56 undergraduate majors (fully accredited): 50 are B.S.; look at list in brochure; must declare a major when applying.
Main focus: career-oriented education, especially in professional and technical fields such as architecture, agriculture, business, computer science, and engineering. Emphasis on undergraduate education; strong support programs in the liberal arts and sciences, with major programs in most traditional arts and science areas (especially Applied Art and Design and Graphic Communication).

General Education is important to all our majors.

Faculty: emphasis on student-centered teaching, student/teacher ratio (18:1), small class size (35 max.), highest persistency rate in the California State University system.

Uniqueness:
"Learn by doing": declare major, hands-on as freshman, labs, co-op, internships, senior project, value to job placement and career.
Student-centered: faculty/staff interest, clubs, organizations, activities, work, involvement, services (advising, learning assistance), Week of Welcome.

V. Applications:

Admissions: California State University application ($55); additional questionnaire due to heavy competition—assures individual attention to each person's qualifications; standards (not for everyone); process; deadlines.

VI. Invitation:

Visit our campus: tours, sit in on classes, counselor appointment (optional), special events, importance and value of visit.
Questions: write for a catalog, write to individual offices, call or write to me (name, office), complete information request card.

VII. Questions and answers: Thank you. "I can stay to answer individual questions."

Chapter 10

Motels, Meals, and Mileage

s you know if you've done any traveling for your university, faculty and staff people who travel on university business are given either a per diem allowance or an expense account to cover the extra cost of eating and sleeping away from home. While we all make jokes about how stingy the allowance is, unless you simply *cannot* be comfortable in anything less than a four-star hotel, your allowance is probably adequate.

Those of us who've been on the road for a number of years have developed lists of preferred motels and restaurants in almost every sector of our territory. Admittedly, there are a few places where there are *no* acceptable accommodations and where the favored local restaurants fall somewhere between Greasy Pete's and Microwave Magic. But with any luck at all, your territory will fall in the more traveler-oriented communities.

Motels

We've all stayed at certain motels that are particularly nice—comfortable and convenient. Sometimes, when you've been on the road for weeks, just the fact that the desk clerk is a motherly soul who sees to it that the coffee pot in the lobby is always full is enough to bring you back year after year.

Sometimes the view or the location makes a motel really special and worth a little extra money, especially if you're going to be camping there for several days. I can't measure the value to me of the seaside location of one of my favorites. An hour sitting on a park bench 80 feet from my motel room, watching sea lions, otters, and gulls, and I'm ready to tackle any kind of challenge the evening program might bring. This kind of experience can make an extended tour away from home seem almost like a vacation, the price of which is only

41

a few hours of work each day. Because of that psychic payoff, I always find the extra dollars involved to be an excellent investment.

On the other end of the spectrum are the overpriced, under-cleaned, noisy places where you never get any rest and never feel good about being there. If you should get stuck in a place like this, I would urge you to move out as soon as possible. It's amazing how sour your general attitude can become just from staying in a sleazy joint while you try to operate as an upbeat professional.

To avoid this kind of hassle in the first place, you might want to check with your outreach staff before you leave campus. Someone has probably been where you're going, and he or she can give you some tips on where to stay. If no one from outreach has been there, the office may have resource people who can help you. Similarly, if you've discovered some little gems on your own travels, don't keep them a secret. There's no such thing as too many perfect places!

Wherever you're going, it's a good idea to phone several days ahead for reservations. Most communities will have lodgings available at any time of the day or night, but unless you enjoy house-hunting at 1 a.m., make a reservation! I'm sure you've had your own unlovely experiences in this realm and that you're not dying to repeat them.

To determine what you can afford in the way of lodging, consider your per diem amount or expense account limit. Subtract the probable cost of two or three meals a day, and what's left is what you can spend on lodging. If you want to stay within your allowance, that is. If you want to put out some extra money of your own and go for the big time, that's up to you. If you end up spending less than your allowance, good for you! You need to check with your outreach office to see whether you get to keep what you saved or whether you have to return all unspent and unaccounted for dollars. Your institution's policy in this matter might determine yours.

One of the most important things to consider when you are selecting overnight accommodations is convenience to your programs. Sometimes, when you're lucky, you can move into a motel, unpack all your stuff, and stay there for the whole week because your programs are all located in the same general area. In fact, some of us incurable homebodies would rather do this and travel 50 miles to a program than keep moving around. Others would rather move to within 10 minutes of the next program and sleep a little later in the morning. Whether you're a "nester" or a "mover" is up to you. Just be sure that you *always* allow for the worst possible traffic conditions between your motel and your morning program so you don't show up for an 8:30 program with 10 o'clock egg on your face.

Meals

If you're one of those truly secure souls who can dine alone in the most elegant restaurants without turning a hair, this section is not for you. You can find a great dinner wherever you are and probably squeeze it into your budget too. However, if you're like most of us, when you're traveling alone, the simple act of feeding yourself can be one of the most threatening events of your day.

The thought of solo dining brings to mind a Steve Martin routine: A man is eating alone in a restaurant when a large spotlight suddenly shines on him and a voice from the darkness says, "Look at that man. He's eating *alone*. There must be something *wrong* with him!" A lot of us feel that way about solo dining. But take heart; there are some basic survival skills that will prevent you from coming back to campus gaunt and emaciated from your travels.

If you are traveling on a circuit of college fairs, you don't need to eat alone. Simply ask a few of the campus reps where they're going and join them. On many of these circuits, lunch is the main meal of the day. The hosts of your morning program will probably serve coffee and pastries before the program, and they're free. So if your system can stand to start each morning with carbohydrates and caffeine, you needn't worry about going out for breakfast. Real dinners are hard to come by when you're spending the hours from 6 to 9 p.m. at a College Night program. Most people are content with a snack when the evening winds down.

I've found that even on our Special trips when I'm traveling alone and I'm at leisure in the evening, I prefer to make lunch my main meal. There are two reasons for this. First, you can eat in the most elegant places at lunchtime for about half what they charge for dinner. Second, there are a lot of "loners" lunching in these places; all sorts of businesspeople have to stop and eat in the middle of the day, so it doesn't feel so lonely in a booth for one as it does in the evening. Just tuck your briefcase or your novel under your arm and walk in as though you owned the joint. You'll find lots of "oners" for company, and the waitresses will be so glad to have something to do along about 2 o'clock that they'll give you fantastic service.

If you're on the road for several days, try not to get carried away with the wondrous variety of rich and forbidden foods available to you. If you stick as closely as reasonably possible to a normal diet, you'll feel much better as the week wears on. Italian food on Monday, Mexican on Tuesday, prime rib on Wednesday, and Chinese on Thursday are not going to do you any favors if your usual fare runs toward meatloaf or macaroni and cheese.

On the topic of things you put in your stomach, take along your pills! Not just the ones you take every day (if you do), but the aspirin and bicarbonate as well. It's easy to get your system out of whack when you're traveling, even if you're trying hard to be good, so you might as well be prepared. You don't have to transport your whole medicine cabinet, but you can figure out the items you might need.

Mileage: Cars and planes

Every college and university has its own set of rules for traveling employees. *Learn them!* You may have thought that travel regulations were not a major

43

area of concern for you, but they are. You can do your job wonderfully and still get tripped up on inadvertent misuse of travel funds or something equally silly. So do learn what your campus policy is regarding travel, both by car and by air.

For example, what will the campus pay for and what are you expected to handle? What if you want to stay a couple of extra days? Are you given a credit card for gas? For telephone? Can you take your spouse with you on a trip in the university car? Will you get per diem or will you be on a voucher basis? If you take your own car, will the university pay you for the mileage? Does the university insure you while you're on the road? In the air? How are travel funds to be obtained, and how are travel expenses to be verified?

Let me say it again: *Learn this stuff.* And find out if there are any more local details you need to know. Not only will this knowledge keep you out of hot water, but it will give you an added sense of confidence as you deal with the nitty-gritties of getting around.

If you're traveling by air, there are some obvious restrictions on how much you can take along, not only for your work, but for yourself. Dozens of trunks and valises may be appropriate traveling gear for someone like Liz Taylor, but remember that she has staff to carry all that stuff from one place to another. As you must survive on a slightly smaller budget, you may want to choose your traveling material for more efficient movement.

First, I would strongly recommend that you take your personal essentials (toothbrush, makeup, one change of clothing, and so on) with you on the plane. The airlines do a remarkable job of getting passengers and their luggage to the same place—most of the time. But unless you're an inveterate gambler, you'll probably feel better knowing you can at least get yourself together when you land in Atlanta, even if your luggage goes on to Miami.

Along with your personal things, take samples of your campus literature in your carry-on bag. Add enough inquiry cards to get you through the first two days of your trip, and you'll be in great shape. Samples and inquiry cards aren't quite the same as a full case of promotional materials, but they're a whole lot better than nothing, and the kids who want to find out all about your institution will feel a lot better about filling out your inquiry cards than they would about your empty hands and charming apology. And they don't need to know that most of your stuff is sitting in the wrong airport.

If you or others on your campus fly a lot as part of your outreach program, you should give serious thought to developing a *small* promotional brochure with an accompanying inquiry card. At the point of first contact, prospective students don't need to know everything about your institution. All they really need is something that will make them want more information. You'll save yourself a lot of backaches if you design a set of promotional literature that can easily be carried around in large quantities.

Here's another thought if you're going to be flying a lot. If you always fly on the same airline, you can be picking up frequent-flyer benefits, and these are yours—not the institution's. Think about it. Why *not* go to Hawaii after a grueling year of flying around the country?

It's a good idea to stay with the same travel agent—not just the same company, but the same person. If your travel agent gets to know you personally, he or she will be likely to spend more time finding you the best possible deals and assuring your convenience and comfort.

When you make reservations for your flight, try to arrange to stay over a Saturday. The price of your ticket goes down dramatically if you do. It's worth it to pay for another night in a hotel with all meals—the savings are that good. Of course, if you are leaving behind a small child or other very significant person, you may not want to spend the extra day away from home, no matter what the dollar cost.

It goes without saying (but I'll say it again anyway) that you should reserve *everything* you're going to use on your trip. Reserve your airline ticket, your motel rooms, your rental car, and anything else you're planning to rent or use temporarily while traveling. And then confirm everything the day before you leave home. This is where your friendly travel agent comes in. You only need to make one phone call to your agent, but be sure your agent makes the other phone calls.

You can make it easier on yourself if you check with your travel agent and your local contact person to see if there are any special events going on in the city you're heading for. If you have any control over *when* you visit an area, you might want to skip the week of the Shriners' convention. They will snap up all the best hotel rooms and rental cars.

And try not to time your arrival to coincide with the morning or afternoon commuter hours. It's hard enough to get your bearings in a strange city without having to shove your rented car through hordes of grim-faced commuters. In fact, if you can manage to arrive about midday the day *before* your obligations begin, you can spend some time learning about the area, resting up, and being good to yourself. Your institution may grumble a bit at this idea, but I'd try for it if I were you. You'll be more effective longer if the frazzle quotient is kept to a minimum.

The last thing I want to mention about flying is, wear comfortable clothes. Your jogging suit would probably be just fine. Plane seats are confining enough without further burdening yourself with belts, straps, high heels, tight jackets, and so forth. On the other hand, if you've inadvertently found yourself in a situation where you have to go directly from the airport to a meeting or presentation, try to wear your most comfortable business clothes. And the business clothes will probably get you better service if you have any difficulties and have to ask for help at the airline counter. So you be the judge.

If you're driving, you might think you have a whole different set of circum-stances. But really, many travel techniques work equally well either way. You still need to wear comfortable clothes while traveling, make all necessary reservations ahead of time and confirm them the day before departure, arrive at your destination before the rush hour, and get some rest before you plunge into your programs.

You need to have a talk with your boss or your campus transportation services department about the restrictions that apply to campus automobiles. It's important to know who can ride in the car with you and who can't, where you can get gas and whether you have to pump it yourself, where you should get the car repaired if you need to and whether you should call the campus first, how far in advance you should reserve your car and for how long a period you can expect to have it. These are such basic bits of knowledge for seasoned travelers that everyone may assume you already know it all, and so they won't bother to tell you. So you'd better ask.

The nice thing about driving is that you get to take more stuff! That can be a blessing or not, depending on how you view your vehicular capacity for abundance. Just remember, you don't have to fill all that space just because it's there. You'll still be better off if you exercise some restraint when packing. As a wise young lady once told me on the way to Europe, "You pack what you're willing to carry, Mom."

In a Nutshell

1. Choose lodging that is safe, pleasant, and convenient to your programs.
2. If you don't know where to stay, ask your outreach office.
3. Make reservations and reconfirm them the day before you leave.
4. Consider making lunch your main meal.
5. When flying, take sample literature and overnight necessities with you on the plane.
6. Use the same travel agent for all your trips and, when possible, the same airline.
7. Travel in comfortable clothes.
8. Time your arrival for minimum traffic hassles and try to give yourself time to regroup before you start working.
9. *Know the travel protocol of your campus.*

The Last Word

Now that you've made your way through this guidebook, you're either dying to get started on your own outreach activities or you're desperately seeking a way out of this whole mess. I hope it's the former, but if outreach isn't your cup of tea after all, don't be embarrassed. A lot of perfectly nice, sane people wouldn't dream of earning their living dashing around the country and talking to a lot of school kids—not even once in a while. But if you decide to keep your outreach guide and give it a whirl, I hope you'll enjoy it, profit by it, and learn from it as well.

In any case, have a good time out there. Drive carefully, be nice to the kids, and take care of yourself.

About the Author

Helen Linstrum is experienced in all aspects of recruitment and admissions. In 1973 she joined admissions at California Polytechnic State University in San Luis Obispo as the first and only admissions counselor. In that position, she wrote and produced almost every brochure, booklet, guide, and form letter that was distributed to prospective students.

She traveled extensively on outreach assignments for about 15 years, both as admissions counselor and later as assistant director of relations with schools. She's been actively involved in Cal Poly's on-campus outreach program of counselor conferences, transfer student days, campus tours, and outreach training programs for faculty and staff. In 1987 she spoke on outreach training at the conference of the Pacific Association of College Registrars and Admissions Officers.

She currently serves as admissions officer for Cal Poly, managing 16 permanent staff members who process approximately 20,000 applications a year on the quarter system.

A native Californian, Linstrum graduated from UCLA in Political Science, taught elementary school for several years, and then earned her M.A. in Education: Counseling and Guidance from Cal Poly. Her present career with Cal Poly began with a two-year stint in the Office of International Education, where she took care of the stateside and on-site needs of six teams of Cal Poly faculty on A.I.D. contracts in Africa, Asia, and Central America.

Notes:

Notes:

Notes:

Notes:

Notes:

Notes: